When the Earth Trembled

A Firsthand Account of Survival, Leadership, and Resilience 25 Years After the 2001 Gujarat Earthquake

Ajay Bhatnagar

Clever Fox® PUBLISHING
Chennai • Bangalore

CLEVER FOX PUBLISHING
Chennai, India

Published by CLEVER FOX PUBLISHING 2026

Paperback ISBN: 978-93-7500-734-0
Hardback ISBN: 978-93-7500-921-4

The author respectfully acknowledges that the events described in this book may revive painful memories for some readers—memories of loss, sorrow, hardship, fear, or the remembrance of loved ones who were lost during that tragic period. If any part of this narrative causes discomfort or rekindles emotions associated with those difficult days, the author offers his sincere apologies.

The purpose of writing this book has never been to reopen wounds or to cause distress. It is solely a personal account of the author's own journey, experiences, and reflections during and after that time. This work is intended as a record of lived moments, resilience, and human response to extraordinary circumstances, shared with humility and respect for all those who were affected.

Images generated using artificial intelligence are used for representation only and do not depict real persons,places,or events unless stated otherwise.

Dedication

I am not sure why, over the last twenty-five years, I never took the initiative to write about an event that changed my life and perspective so profoundly. Yet, in time, it seemed destined that I would finally pen down my unforgettable experiences.

The beginning of this journey as an author is deeply rooted in the unwavering encouragement of my wife, **Manisha Bhatnagar**. She stood beside me during one of the most devastating periods of our lives—the earthquake—and continued to stand with me every single day thereafter. Her strength, resilience, and quiet support have been my constant source of stability, both in life and in this endeavour. Without her faith and encouragement, this book would never have taken shape.

I am equally indebted to my daughter, **Dr Aastha Bhatnagar**, whose motivation, insight, and relentless commitment transformed this manuscript into a finished work. Her sharp eye for detail, repeated and meticulous proof-reading, thoughtful suggestions, and careful formatting elevated the narrative and ensured its clarity and readability. More than a contributor, she became a guiding force in this journey, ensuring that every page reached its rightful conclusion.

This book carries within it not just my experiences, but also the silent strength, patience, and dedication of the two people who made its completion possible.

With the constant support of my family, I was able to bring this book to life. I gratefully dedicate this book to my revered mentor, **Late Dr N. V. Nayak**, whose guidance, wisdom, and values played a defining role in shaping my professional journey.

Dr N. V. Nayak was a true visionary and an exceptional mentor. He listened patiently, understood problems in their entirety, and offered timely solutions—whether the challenges were technical, administrative, or even deeply personal. His clarity of thought, compassion, and decisive leadership left an indelible impression on my life, for which I remain eternally grateful.

Through this book, I also wish to express my heartfelt gratitude to all my seniors, colleagues, and co-workers for their unwavering support and dedication. Their collective efforts, especially during the most challenging circumstances, made it possible to overcome every hurdle. Without their support, this journey—and this book—would not have been possible.

Acknowledgements

It would be incomplete to narrate my professional journey without acknowledging the invaluable guidance of my seniors, who played a pivotal role in shaping my career. I humbly express my deep gratitude to the following mentors who guided me with wisdom and integrity:

Late Shri Dr N. V. Nayak
Late Shri C. Bhattacharjee
Late Shri N. K. Bhatia
Late Shri N. K. Chowdhary
Shri M. U. Shah
Shri A. B. Desai
Shri K. N. Chatterjee

I remain in touch with Shri M. U. Shah and Shri K. N. Chatterjee, whose mentorship continues to inspire me even today. From each of my mentors, I learned invaluable lessons that shaped my professional conduct and strengthened my technical judgment.

It goes without saying that the journey from a Junior Engineer to a Project Manager cannot be achieved through individual effort alone. It requires the collective support of colleagues, junior staff, supervisors, administrative teams, and countless workers who contribute tirelessly behind the scenes. Their dedication and cooperation made it possible to deliver complex projects under challenging conditions.

I express my heartfelt gratitude to all colleagues, workers, service providers, and administrative staff who stood by me throughout my career. I also acknowledge with deep respect **Shri Abhijit Rajan**, the Chairman and Managing Director of Gammon India Limited, who appointed me as a permanent employee in 1993 and later honoured me with a promotion to Project Manager. I still preserve the appointment letter signed by him, which remains one of my most cherished professional possessions.

Preface

It has been a quarter of a century since the most devastating earthquake struck the Kutch region at 8:46 a.m. on 26th January 2001. Since it is an event that one can never forget, even across several lifetimes, it remained somewhere in the back of my mind while I continued with the routine responsibilities of life, earning my livelihood and supporting my family.

Post my daughter's marriage recently , when I finally stepped away from active service, I found myself with some quiet moments to reflect. It was during this time that memories began to resurface, and with the encouragement of my wife, I gathered the courage to relive and document my experiences during and after the earthquake—memories that still haunt me deeply.

This is my first attempt at writing. Through these pages, I have tried to capture some of the most horrifying and unforgettable moments of my life. Of course there were the moments of joy, happiness and deep satisfaction also and If my words are able to touch even a few hearts, I will consider my effort worthwhile. With the blessings of my readers, I hope to continue writing about similar real-life experiences that occurred at different project sites during my 34 years of service.

Contents

Chapter One

The Great Rann of Kutch

The White Desert of Kutch, also known as the Great Rann of Kutch, is a vast salt marsh located in the Kutch district of Gujarat, India.

Fig: I.1 Aerial view of Rann of Kutch

It is one of the most unique geographical regions of the country, known for its striking landscape and ecological significance.

Hadakiya Creek, situated in Gujarat's Kachchh district, is a lesser-known yet remarkable natural feature along India's western coastline. It provides a natural habitat for a wide variety of migratory shorebirds and supports a rich and diverse ecosystem.

The Suraj Bari mudflats, located in the western part of the Little Rann of Kutch, form an important ecological zone. Tidal waters from the Gulf of Kutch enter through the Hadakiya Creek and flow through a network of channels extending nearly 3–4 kilometres into the Rann.

Salt panning is a vital seasonal activity in the Rann of Kutch and contributes significantly to India's inland salt production. During the monsoon season, the underground water table rises, filling the region with saline water and creating vast salt flats once the water evaporates.

The 2001 Gujarat earthquake, also known as the Bhuj earthquake, occurred on 26 January at 08:46 am IST. The epicentre was about 9 km south-southwest of the village of Chobari in Bhachau Taluka of Kutch.

The moment magnitude of the quake was 7.7 (6.9 on the Richter scale) with stronger ground motion lasting at least 85 seconds. Numerous rockfalls and landslides occurred in the Bhuj and Bhachau areas.

There was extensive evidence of soil liquefaction at the Rann of Kutch, and in the coastal areas of the Gulf of Kutch and numerous sand boils in dry lakebeds northeast of Bhuj. After the earthquake, these sand boils had fountains of saline groundwater rising 2–3 meters.

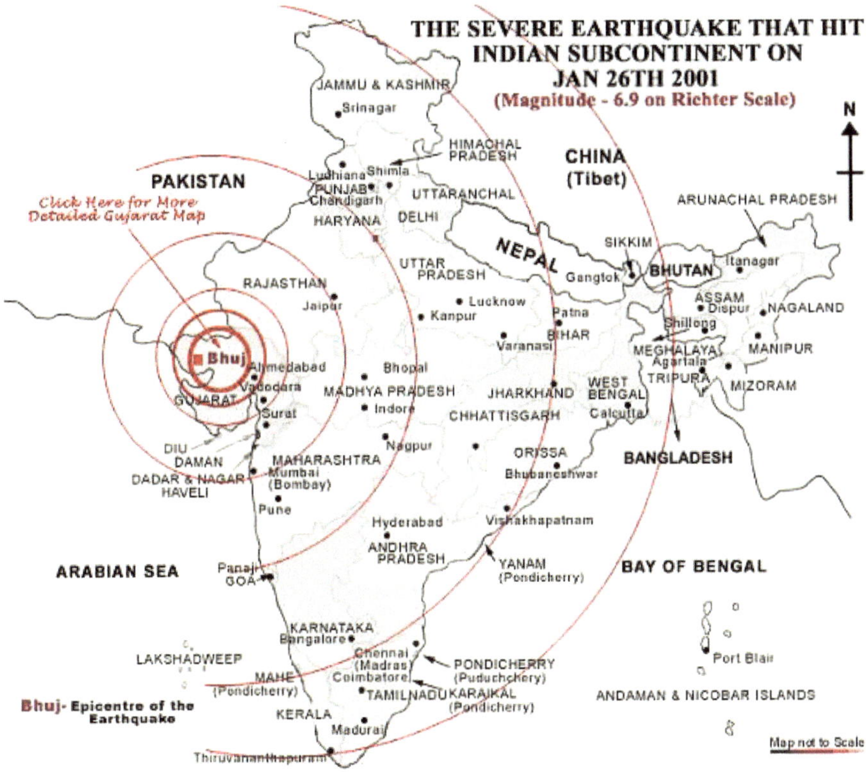

Fig:I.2

The earthquake was caused by movement on a previously unknown south-dipping fault, trending parallel to the inferred rift structures. No major surface ruptures were associated with the shock, classifying it as a blind thrust earthquake.

The earthquake killed at least 20,000 people, injured another around 164,000 and destroyed about 400,000 buildings in Gujarat, India and Sindh, Pakistan. The vast majority of deaths and damage were observed in Kutch district, while nearly 1,600 additional deaths occurred in other cities of Gujarat

Chapter Two

My Journey to the Suraj Bari Creek Bridge

As mentioned in the previous chapter, I began my professional journey in 1991 with the Sikar–Pilani Road Project.

From there, I was transferred to the Almatti Dam project in Karnataka in 1993. In mid-1996, my services were again transferred—this time to the construction of the new Note Press Project at Salboni, Midnapore, West Bengal, where I worked as a Section-in-Charge.

The details of these individual projects are stories in themselves and deserve separate narration. However, as the focus of this book is the Suraj Bari Creek Bridge, I shall refrain from elaborating on them here.

In those days, the organisational structure was very systematic. The Project Head reported directly to the Contract Management Section (CMS), and all project-related matters were routed through this hierarchy. The system functioned with clarity and discipline, and everyone was expected to work strictly within defined roles and responsibilities.

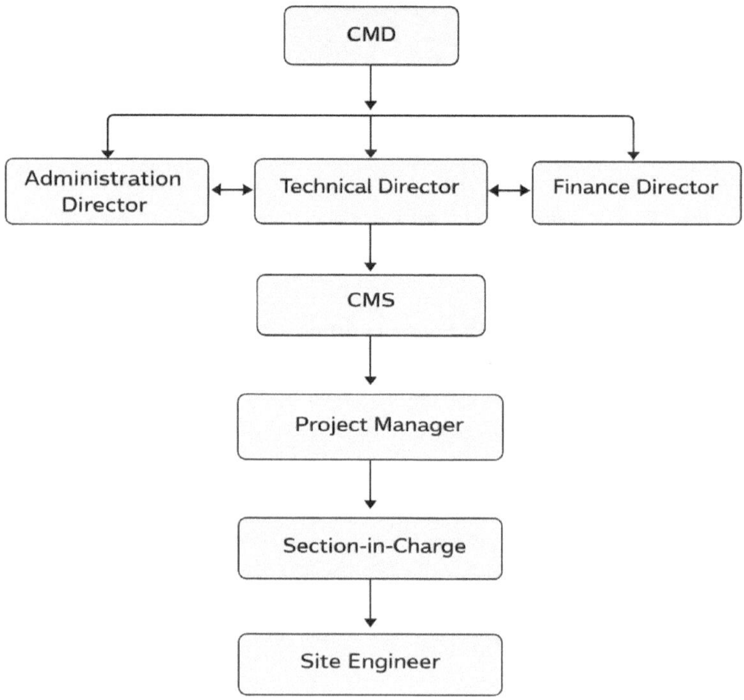

Fig:II.1 Organisational Hierarchy

When I joined the Salboni project, I was assigned to the precast yard as deputy Section-in-Charge.

The precast yard was most vital and the backbone of the project, as it handled the casting of various structural components such as beams and roofing elements in a factory-like environment, operating round the clock throughout the year.

After about a year, my Section-in-Charge received orders transferring him to the Suraj Bari Creek Bridge project. We bid him farewell, unaware that fate had already decided my future path.

At that time, I had no idea that one day I would also be posted to the same project, where some of the most defining moments of my life would unfold.

Following his transfer, I was entrusted with the responsibility of Section-in-Charge of the precast yard, a role I had earlier supported as second-in-command. It was another turning point in my career.

Once again, destiny played its silent role. The very officer who handed over the precast yard to me before leaving for the Suraj Bari Creek Bridge would, in the years to come, hand over to me the responsibility of that very project as Project Manager.

After taking charge, work resumed at a steady pace. With the guidance of my seniors and the collective efforts of the team, we achieved our production targets successfully. In recognition of my performance, I was promoted to the post of Senior Engineer. During this period, my daughter also began her schooling, joining LKG in the same CISF-protected township where we were residing as part of the Gammon family.

Life continued smoothly until October 1998, when I received my transfer order to move to the Suraj Bari Creek Bridge project. This came as a surprise, as the precast yard work was still ongoing. Nevertheless, the instructions came directly from the Head Office, leaving no scope for delay or discussion.

At that time, opportunities were limited, and there was no internet or easy access to information. Unlike today, where opportunities are visible at the click of a button, those days demanded discipline, patience, and complete commitment to organisational decisions. We accepted transfers as part of professional duty, without hesitation.

Once the transfer order was received, my wife and I began packing our belongings. As was customary then, accommodation was provided by the company, and all furniture issued had to be returned to the project site store before relocation. The same procedure applied whenever one moved to a new project.

As I prepared for the move, I attempted to book train tickets from Midnapore to Gujarat. However, fate had its own plans. It was the festive season of Durga Puja, and train tickets were unavailable. Despite multiple attempts, I could not secure confirmed reservations.

Faced with this situation, I decided to travel via Mumbai, hoping that from there it would be easier to reach Bhachau by train or bus. Unfortunately, that plan too did not work out as expected.

After reaching Mumbai, we stayed with a family friend who had earlier worked with me at the Salboni project and had since been transferred to a Mumbai assignment. Even from Mumbai, securing travel arrangements proved difficult.

The next morning, driven by urgency and uncertainty, I decided to visit the project site where my colleague was posted at the Mankhurd Flyover. As I stood there, I had no idea that what awaited me next would become one of the most defining moments of my life.

Just then, the Director from Head Office—who had instructed my transfer to the Suraj Bari Creek project—arrived at the site for an inspection. To my utter surprise, he noticed me there.

With trembling legs, upon his calling I approached him, expecting a stern reprimand. He looked at me and asked sharply,
"Why are you here? You should have been at the Suraj Bari site by now."

Gathering all my courage, I explained that I was travelling with my wife and daughter and had been unable to secure confirmed tickets. The Director listened patiently, paused for a moment, and then instructed his assistant to arrange air tickets for me and my family from Mumbai to Bhuj, the nearest airport to project site.

I was stunned. Air travel was something I had never experienced before, and it was completely beyond my expectations and eligibility as well. His gesture reflected not only authoritative but deep empathy and leadership too. He also instructed that transport also be arranged from Bhuj airport to project site, nearly 140 kilometres away.

A First Flight and an Unexpected Encounter

The sudden opportunity to travel by air—for the first time in our lives—filled both my wife and me with a strange mix of excitement, curiosity, and disbelief. Until then, flying was something we had only seen in films or heard others speak about.

Now, without any preparation or expectation, we found ourselves stepping into an unfamiliar world that felt both thrilling and overwhelming.

As we sat together, our conversation flowed endlessly—wondering how it would feel when the aircraft took off, whether the sound would be frightening, how the land below would appear once we were airborne, and whether we would feel any discomfort in our ears or will our daughter be comfortable.

Every announcement, every movement at the airport, and every sight through the glass windows sparked fresh curiosity.

Amid this innocent excitement, we noticed a young man standing alone with his cricket kit at the Mumbai airport—simple, composed, and unassuming. It was **Rahul Dravid**, then an upcoming cricketer, waiting quietly without any crowd or attention around him.

At that moment, we could not have imagined that this young man would one day become one of the most respected and celebrated figures in Indian cricket.

Fig: II.2 First Flight (Concept visualization created using AI)

That journey—our **first flight**, our shared excitement, and the unexpected sight of a future legend—remains etched in my memory.

It reminded me that life often gifts us extraordinary moments in the most ordinary settings.

This is how I finally reached the Suraj Bari Creek project site — the place where history awaited me.

The ***Suraj Bari Creek Bridge*** is located across the Great Rann of Kutch on the Kandla Road, forming part of the national highway network.

The bridge was first constructed in 1968. During the 1965 war with Pakistan, the strategic importance of providing a reliable road connection between Kutch and the rest of India was strongly realized.

Following the construction of the bridge, the economic and social development of the region improved significantly.

Keeping in view the growing strategic and economic requirements, it was later decided to construct a new Suraj Bari Creek Bridge in the upstream of the existing structure.

This new bridge was planned to enhance connectivity and support increasing traffic demands.

The Suraj Bari Bridge is located approximately 43 kilometres from Bhachau-the epicentre of Earthquake.

Others Distances from major cities of Gujarat

Gandhinagar – 230 km
Rajkot – 111 km
Kandla Port – 95 km
Bhuj – 138 km

*Fig:II.3 Road map with Suraj Bari marked as star **

Chapter Three

An Overview of the Project

The geographical details of the Suraj Bari Creek have already been described in the earlier chapter. Therefore, this section focuses on the project itself and its structural aspects.

The Suraj Bari Creek Bridge project was awarded to **Gammon India Limited** by the Public Works Department (PWD) of Gujarat, headquartered at Gandhidham.

The project was not executed under FIDIC conditions; hence, no Project Management Consultant (PMC) was appointed. Gammon India Limited being the main contractor, while the PWD served as the client and supervising authority as well.

The project followed the EPC (Engineering, Procurement, and Construction) model, with all designs prepared by the in-house design team at the Head Office of Gammon India Limited.

The approved GFC (Good for Construction) drawings were then issued to the site for execution.

Major Components of the Bridge

A. The permanent structural components of the bridge includes:

a.) Circular Well Foundation

b.) Well Caps

c.) Well Piers

d.) Abutment Cap and Piers

e.) Pier Caps

f.) Superstructure

f.1) I Girders

f.2) RCC Deck Slab

f.3) Bituminous Carpeting

g.) Approach slab

h.) Approach roads

B. The temporary structure and other establishments includes:

a.) Pre-Casting Yard

b.) Project office ,Stores and other establishments like QC lab, Plant and equipment room etc.

c.) Concrete Mix Plant

d.) Staff Colony &

e.) Labour Colony etc.

To expedite construction, it was decided to cast **pre-stressed, pre-tensioned 32-metre-long I-girders**. For this purpose, a dedicated casting yard was established.

Following are the original pictures of precast yard.

Fig:III.1

Fig:III.2

Fig:III.3

Within the organisation, I was entrusted with the responsibility of serving as **Section-in-Charge of the casting yard**.

This role involved overseeing the production of I-girders, which was both technically demanding and time-sensitive.

To meet project requirements, a steam curing system was installed, complete with boilers and supporting infrastructure, to ensure consistent quality and strength development of the concrete elements.

The launching of the girders were carried out using heavy-duty Goliath gantries and specialised SICET launching equipment.

Fig:III.4 Erection of Girder by Gantries

Fig:III.5 Erection of Girder by Sicet

Fig:III.6 Erection of Girder by Sicet

Temporary jetties were constructed to facilitate the movements and for the placement of the precast girders over the pier caps.

Fig:III.7 Construction activities over temporary Jetty

FiG:III.8 Making of temporary jetty in progress

Supporting facilities such as the site office, stores, labour colony, and staff accommodation were all established in close proximity to the project site, enabling smooth coordination and efficient execution of work.

Seeking Blessings from the Divine Engineer

Apart from our regular construction activities, the celebration of **Lord Vishwakarma Pooja** was always a significant annual event. Like all construction companies, we observed this sacred occasion to seek blessings from **Lord Vishwakarma**, revered as the Divine Engineer, whose grace we believed guided our work and protected those engaged in it.

The celebration brought everyone together in faith and gratitude, reinforcing the bond between effort and belief that sustained us through demanding times.

Presented here are photographs from the **Vishwakarma Pooja celebration held on 17th September 2000**, capturing moments of devotion, unity, and reverence at the project site.

Fig:III.9

Fig:III.10

Fig:III.11

Chapter Four

The Role of Project Management

After joining the Suraj Bari Creek Bridge project in October 1998, I was residing in a small town called Samakhiyali, about 26 kilometres from the project site—a journey of approximately 35 minutes by road. The district headquarters, Bhachau, where my daughter attended St. Xavier's School, was about 20 kilometres away from Samakhiali.

Although a staff colony had been constructed near the project site, my daughter was too young to travel daily from the colony to Bhachau. Therefore, with the permission of the then Project-in-Charge, I continued to stay in a rented accommodation—a G+2 building—in Samakhiyali. The importance of sharing these details are relevant and will reveal in the later chapters.

As fate would have it, after nearly two years at the project, I received a message asking me to contact the Director. By that time, I had been promoted to the position of Project Engineer. When I called him, he said simply, "Bhatnagar, you have to take charge of the project now. Can you handle it?"

I was taken completely by surprise. At that time, I was still relatively junior in the organisational hierarchy, and the responsibility being offered was far greater than what I had anticipated.

Hesitantly, I responded- "Sir, existing Project Manager is required as the project is at very crucial stage".

He immediately replied, "We are transferring him to another project. Can you handle this responsibility?"

With a mix of nervousness and determination, I replied, "Yes, Sir. With your guidance, I will manage."

That was it. The call ended.

I stood there in silence for a few moments, trying to absorb what had just happened. Being entrusted with such responsibility at an early stage of my career felt both overwhelming and deeply rewarding.

The formal process soon followed. The Project Manager, who had earlier served as my Section-in-Charge and later as Project Manager, handed over charge to me. Once again, destiny had played its quiet role in shaping my journey.

Fig:IV.1 Handing Over

In August 2000, I officially assumed the role of Project Manager.

With the increase in responsibilities, I decided to shift from my rented accommodation in Samakhiyali to the staff colony closer to the project site. Although this meant that my young daughter would have to travel a longer distance to school, my wife and daughter accepted the situation with remarkable understanding and support.

By then, the project was progressing steadily, with the main bridge targeted for completion by the first week of March 2001, and the entire project scheduled for completion by June 2001.

Chapter Five

The Day the earth shook

On 25th January 2001, I travelled to Gandhinagar, covering a distance of approximately 225 kilometres. The journey took nearly six hours. I was accompanied by the Assistant Executive Engineer of the PWD, as we had an official meeting scheduled with senior officers from the Head Office.

Before leaving the project site, I instructed my deputy that since I would be returning late at night, arrangements should be made for the Republic Day flag-hoisting ceremony the following morning. I also clearly mentioned that, even being 26th January, a national holiday the workers should resume work after the ceremony, as we were under immense pressure to meet the project deadline and could not afford any delay.

At that moment, I had no idea that this single instruction would save many lives the very next day.

After a long and tiring journey, we returned late at night. I arranged for the Assistant Executive Engineer to be dropped at his residence in Bhachau, which was about 45 kilometres from Suraj Bari, after reaching my place. It was nearly 2:30 a.m. by the time I reached home

The night passed quietly. **On the morning of 26th January 2001**—a date that would be etched forever in history—I woke up around 7:00 a.m. Since it was Republic Day, only a flag-hoisting ceremony was scheduled at my daughter's school. I advised my wife that it would be better if our daughter did not go to school that day, as the distance was long and our driver had already been exhausted from the previous night's travel.

Little did I know that this decision would save my daughter's life.

After finishing my morning routine, I was preparing to leave for the project site. At around 8:45 a.m., while I was shaving, I suddenly felt the ground tremble beneath my feet.

For a moment, I froze.

Within seconds, I saw the Tata Sumo parked outside my house shaking violently. In that instant, I realised the magnitude of what was happening. I grabbed my daughter, shouted to my wife, "Run outside! It's an earthquake!" and rushed out of the house.

The entire area was in chaos. The ground shook violently, vehicles rocked, dust and sand rose from the earth, and people screamed in panic. The colony was filled with fear and confusion.

Composure in the midst of fear

Despite the fear gripping my own heart, I had to gather myself. As the person in charge of the project, I knew I had a responsibility toward everyone around me. I first ensured the safety of my family and then began calming the residents and staff who had assembled outside.

Although fear was overwhelming, I forced myself to stay composed. My immediate concern was to assess the damage and ensure that no one went back inside the buildings, as aftershocks were still occurring.

I quickly instructed everyone to remain in open areas and contacted my assistant, directing him to keep everyone together. The tremors continued intermittently, reminding us that the danger had not yet passed.

Only later did we realise that the earthquake had measured 7.7 on the Richter scale and that the destruction across the region was far beyond anything we could have imagined.

Chapter Six

The Impact of the Earthquake

At around 10:00 a.m., I began assessing the condition of the staff colony before moving further. Most of the houses had developed deep cracks in the walls.

In many places, the roofs made of CGI sheets had shifted, and the ground itself had cracked open, with water and sand oozing out. The sight was terrifying beyond words.

As I prepared to move out in my Tata Sumo, my young daughter, still shaken with fear, insisted on accompanying me. Seeing the fear in her eyes, I could not refuse.

Our first stop was the project site. What we witnessed there was nothing short of devastation. The entire area looked as though it had been ravaged by a powerful force of nature.

The approach roads to the bridge had sunk at several locations. Out of the 39 erected spans, 37 had been displaced from their bearings, crashing against the seismic stoppers.

Had these stoppers not been in place, the entire bridge could have collapsed.

The labour colony had also suffered extensive damage.

Fig:VI.1: 1 meter wide longitudinal cracks in the embankment

Fig:VI.2: Damaged seismic barrier due to lateral movement of bridge span

Fig:VI.3: View of sand boils

I thanked God from the depths of my heart that we had instructed the workers to report to duty early that morning. Had they been inside their quarters at the time of the earthquake, the loss of life would have been unimaginable.

A kind gesture

While I was trying to get a hang of what had transpired to the site I was responsible for, my daughter, a six year old little girl, waited for my return anxiously in the safety of our car.

An incident, she frequently fondly recollects was of a neighbourhood shopkeeper, who approached her as she waited for me to return from the site.

It was that uncertain period of aftershocks, where within a few minutes you couldn't think what your next move should be, whether to abandon the area, leaving everything behind, all your belongings, earnings, assets or to stay and wait for what's going to come.

Being a small shop owner back then, were difficult times, with not so much wealth that would need a bank account or savings in gold, all they had, was the shop and the things they had kept in it, to sell.

This particular shopkeeper had spiralled into the panic mode, to leave everything behind and save his life, for what it was worth. After drawing the shutter to his shop, one last time,

He came in a frenzy, frightened, near the car, looked at the frightened face of my six-year-old daughter, through the passenger side window of my SUV, handed her a neat box of chocolates, uttering **"god bless you, beti"** while caressing the side of her face with his trembling hands and wet eyes, as if to say, this is all I had, gone in a single day, in an event, that literally displaced the ground beneath us.

Everytime my daughter would recall the incident, she would end up describing it with more detail and adding her own outlook of the situation as her experiences grew. But this incident has haunted her as much as she cherishes the fond memories of the same wishing well for the shopkeeper and his family.

It is instances like these, where one would start thinking about their savings, wealth, earnings and how we could be ripped of all our assets in the blink of an eye.

This is where your faith is tested, your beliefs shaken, could either leave a human closer to the ultimate power or force him to turn away from the concept of it all together.

In the case of my daughter, her faith strengthened, in the case of the shopkeeper, only he would know. But such is life where the same moment can drift people in two different directions, by which, I am in no ways, hinting at him growing apart, just a simple possibility.

Fig:VI.4 A kind gesture (Concept visualization created using AI)

After assessing the site, we proceeded towards the district headquarters at Bhachau, which we later learned was the epicentre of the earthquake. What we witnessed there was beyond description.

Entire neighbourhoods were flattened. Walls had collapsed, roads had cracked open, and electric poles lay twisted on the ground. People were screaming for help, searching for loved ones amid the rubble.

Holding my daughter tightly, I stood frozen, unable to comprehend the scale of devastation. It was a scene no human heart could easily bear.

Fig:VI.5,

Fig:VI.6,

Fig:VI.7,

Fig:VI.8

After gathering myself, I decided to search for a public call office (PCO) to inform the authorities and seek assistance. However, no PCO was operational, and there was no one available to help. We then moved towards Samakhiyali, the place where I had previously stayed before shifting to the staff colony.

The situation there was no different. Destruction was everywhere. Eventually, I managed to locate a working PCO in Maliya Miyana, about 15 kilometres away from project site.

From there, I contacted the Head Office and informed them about the catastrophe. I requested immediate support, including tents and essential supplies for staff and workers who were now homeless.

The Head Office had already begun receiving information through news channels, but my call helped them understand the gravity of the situation on the ground. They assured me that all possible assistance would be extended, which indeed arrived in the days that followed.

A Goodbye Never Meant to Be Final

The Assistant Executive Engineer (AEE) of the Public Works Department—our client and supervising authority—had travelled with me to Gandhinagar on 25th January 2001 for an official meeting. We returned together in the same vehicle in the early hours of the following day.

On reaching my residence at the company's staff colony around 2:30 a.m. on 26th January, I requested my driver to drop the AEE at his home in Bhachau, nearly 45 kilometres away.

I wished him good night and a happy weekend and walked into my house—never imagining, even for a fraction of a second, that these would be my last words to him.

My driver drove on, dropped the AEE at his residence in Bhachau, and returned around 4:30 a.m., after which he went straight home to rest. After the earthquake struck and everything lay in chaos, we travelled to Bhachau to assess the situation. We decided to visit the AEE's house to enquire about the well-being of him and his family, and also to update him with a first-hand account of the damage sustained at the project site.

It would have been far better had I not gone there.

When we reached his house, we found his wife crying helplessly, desperately seeking assistance to retrieve her husband, who had been trapped inside their collapsed home. As we tried to console her, she narrated—through tears and a trembling voice—that the moment they felt their house shaking, the AEE pushed her out to safety. Just as he was about to step out himself, the entire structure collapsed, trapping him beneath the debris.

Later, with the help of a JCB and other means, we were able to recover only his lifeless body.

What a loss. A man lost his life while saving his soulmate—standing against the cruelty of nature, and giving his life in that very act.

Some sacrifices do not happen on battlefields; they happen quietly, within the walls of a home, and are remembered forever.

Fig:VI.9 (Concept visualization created using AI)

Gone Before Dawn

Another engineer from the Public Works Department, entrusted with quality control responsibilities, also lost his life when the roof of his house collapsed while he lay asleep. He never had a moment to realise what was happening, nor a chance to escape.

The silence of the night was broken by destruction, and by morning, another life had been cruelly taken away.

This loss shook us deeply. The swiftness with which life had been erased left us numb.

It was not merely the loss of a colleague, but the painful reminder of how fragile human existence truly is when confronted by nature's unforgiving force.

The grief lingered in silence, long after the tremors had ceased.

Devastation

In Kutch District, 90% of homes were damaged or destroyed, with 24% of the housing stock affected overall in Gujarat; most affected buildings were non-engineered, unreinforced stonemasonry, although many reinforced concrete buildings also collapsed.

Water outages were widespread due to liquefaction and soil compaction, with many pumping stations and two water towers collapsing in the affected area. However, damages to highways and bridges were relatively minor.

Bhuj, one of the closest city to the epicentre, was devastated with 95% of buildings destroyed or uninhabitable after the quake.

Adirondack Daily Enterprise • Saturday, January 27, 2001 • A7

International News

India struck by massive quake; over 2,000 dead

By NIRMALA GEORGE
Associated Press Writer

AHMEDABAD, India (AP) – The most powerful earthquake to strike India in a half century rocked the subcontinent Friday, killing more than 2,000 people, injuring 3,000 and leaving desperate survivors clawing through the rubble of collapsed buildings in search of loved ones.

The 7.9 magnitude temblor in western Gujarat state, close to the border with Pakistan, shook high-rise towers 600 miles away in the capital, New Delhi. The quake could be felt as far as 1,200 miles away in Calcutta and coastal Bangladesh – a distance about equivalent to that between Washington and Dallas.

"The earthquake is a calamity of national magnitude," Indian Prime Minister Atal Bihari Vajpayee said. "We have decided to meet the emergency on a war footing. This is the time for people to rally around."

The quake struck at 8:50 a.m. (10:20 p.m. EST Thursday) as many cities were beginning celebrations for India's 51st Republic Day, which commemorates the adoption of the country's constitution. In Ahmedabad, Gujarat's commercial capital and a sprawling city of 4.5 million, helmeted rescue workers used iron rods to pry slabs of concrete and metal, searching for survivors. Women wept and rocked back and forth, watching as the few available bulldozers and cranes pushed through the piles of stone that once had housed families and shops.

Beds, children's toys and clothes lay abandoned in the debris, lamp posts and electric pylons were twisted and many buildings were left leaning precariously.

After night fell, with temperatures at 55 degrees, survivors spread blankets and huddled around campfires.

"There is a great panic among the people and they have spilled out onto the streets," said Haren Panya, home minister of Gujarat. Because of the aftershocks, "We have asked people to move out of old buildings."

The 2,063 deaths in India were all recorded in Gujarat state – including hundreds in Ahmedabad – where buildings swayed for more than two minutes, said P.I. Kanpuri, a police officer at the emergency state control room in Gandhinagar, the state capital. Ten people died in Pakistan when two houses collapsed.

The tremors shook across much of the north and west of this vast nation of one billion people, and even extended to the mountains of Nepal, 1,000 miles north of the epicenter. Authorities in India said 3,200 people were injured. No damage or injuries were reported in the rest of India.

The epicenter was near Bhuj, a desert town of 150,000 people in Gujarat. Ninety percent of the houses in Bhuj were damaged, said Cabinet minister Pramod Mahajan. Kanpuri said 1,400 people in Bhuj district had been killed.

The area was plunged into darkness. At least four planes carrying soldiers, paramedics, food, medicine and tents landed at Bhuj's Air Force base, said R. K. Dhinga, an air force spokesman, in New Delhi.

Bhuj's main hospital, run by the air force, was crammed with seriously injured people. Nearly 1,000 injured residents, most wrapped in blankets against the night chill, were camping outside the hospital waiting their turn, the Star television network reported.

The quake did no damage to the two 220-megawatt nuclear plants in Gujarat, authorities said. But gas pipelines, most power supply stations, phone lines and water service were knocked out across the arid state, which is prone to drought.

In Ahmedabad, a center of India's textile industry, as many as 50 multistory buildings crumbled. Hundreds of people besieged the fire station asking for help to dig out their relatives, said fire chief Rajesh Bhat.

"This is an emergency. We are facing a riotous crowd," Bhat said. "A fear psychosis is developing in the city. People have fled their homes and are taking refuge in open fields."

Corpses were piled up on the verandah of the N.S. Hospital, while patients overflowing into the hallways wailed and screamed with broken limbs and bleeding wounds. Press Trust of India reported 70 people died awaiting treatment.

Bruised and bleeding bodies were laid in rows, covered with blankets as relatives sat by mourning.

The Indian government said it was flying 10,000 tents, 10,000 tons of grain, 20 doctors and surgeons, communications and seismology experts to Gujarat. Vajpayee sent his home minister, Lal K. Advani, who said the death toll "could be 1,000 or more."

Vajpayee made no appeal for international aid, saying those needs were being assessed.

President Bush, the United Nations, and Pakistan's army ruler Gen. Pervez Musharraf sent condolences. Bush said the United States is willing to provide assistance if needed, and the U.N. Office for the Coordination of Humanitarian Assistance announced that it will send a five-member earthquake assesment team to India on Sunday.

The quake was the most powerful to strike India since Aug. 15, 1950, when an 8.5 magnitude temblor killed 1,538 people in northeastern Assam state.

Fig:VI.10

The New York Times

Late Edition
New York: Today, cloudy, few snow showers, high 40. Tonight, clearing, windy, low 29. Tomorrow, mostly sunny, cool, high 38. Yesterday, high 36, low 21. Weather map on Page D8.

NEW YORK, SATURDAY, JANUARY 27, 2001 — 75 CENTS

GIULIANI TO SHIFT POLICE DISCIPLINE TO CIVILIAN BOARD

MAJOR CHANGE PROPOSED

Cost of a Switch Is Unclear — Mayor's Critics Laud Move but Unions Are Dubious

By WILLIAM K. RASHBAUM and KEVIN FLYNN

Mayor Rudolph W. Giuliani announced yesterday that police officers accused of misconduct would no longer be prosecuted by the Police Department, but by the independent agency that evaluates civilian complaints of abuse.

The mayor offered few details about the changes, and city officials said it would take months before any plan could be put into place. Still, it represents a major turnabout for the mayor, once one of the harshest critics of civilian oversight of the police.

The agency, the Civilian Complaint Review Board, would be given expanded powers to charge and prosecute officers that it found had committed misconduct. The Police Department currently prosecutes these cases, which are referred by the review board, a process that has come under fire both from critics of the department and from officers.

Critics have said that police prosecutors too often fail to act on bona fide cases referred by the review board. In particular federal prosecu-

Severe Earthquake Strikes India, Killing Thousands

A crowd gathered yesterday outside a building that collapsed in Ahmedabad, India, as a result of the powerful earthquake that struck the area.

Fig:VI.11

Fig:VI.12

Over 1.2 million houses in 8,000 villages and 490 towns were damaged or destroyed, as well as 12,000 schools, 2,000 health facilities, many historic buildings and tourist attractions

Chapter Seven

When God Protected Us

After witnessing the massive destruction caused by the earthquake, I was filled with a strange mix of shock and gratitude.

On one hand, the devastation was beyond imagination; on the other, I felt deeply blessed, as several decisions taken unknowingly in the past had saved not only my life but the lives of many others as well.

Incident 1 – A Home Reduced to Silence

While returning from Bhachau on the day the earth trembled with a heavy heart, a quiet voice rose from deep within me, urging me to check the condition of Samakhiyali, the place that had once been my home during the early months of my posting at the Suraj Bari Creek Bridge Project.

As mentioned earlier, we had lived there in a rented G+2 structure. The ground floor housed a small shop run by the owner, Mr Bachchu Bhai, while my family and I occupied the upper floors.

As I drew closer to the locality, my heart began to sink. Most of the buildings lining the road were badly damaged, scarred by destruction, and the surroundings carried an eerie silence that felt deeply unsettling.

Yet, summoning what little courage I had, I pushed myself forward towards my former residence. When I finally reached the spot, I was confronted with a scene I would never have wished to witness—even in my worst nightmares.

The entire building had been reduced to rubble and dust. One could only imagine the fate of those who might have been inside. Being a standalone structure, all the walls, along with the roof, had completely collapsed.

To my profound sorrow, the water tank that once stood atop the roof lay helplessly rolling on the road. Tears welled up in my eyes. The whole building had flattened like a thin sheet of paper.

This was the very place where I had spent several happy months with my family—where laughter once echoed, and where I often exchanged warm, casual conversations with Bachchu Bhai while coming home or leaving for work.

Sometime later, I met Bachchu Bhai again in the village. To my utter disbelief, I could barely recognise him. The once cheerful, witty man now stood before me as someone who seemed to have lost all interest in life.

He had grown visibly thinner, and it felt as though I was speaking to a completely different person. During our conversation of nearly fifteen minutes, I did not see even the faintest hint of a smile on his face—whereas earlier, he would smile or laugh wholeheartedly even during the smallest exchanges.

It was a living testament to how a sudden and merciless calamity can alter lives forever, through no fault of those who suffer it. The pain was real, deep, and impossible to forget.

At that moment, only the thought came in my mind — **had we still been living there, none of us would have survived. It was then that I truly realised how divine intervention had protected my family.**

Incident 2 – A Hint That Saved a Life

I clearly remember that when I returned home in the early hours of 26th January 2001 from Gandhinagar, after a hectic meeting and an exhausting journey,

I spoke to my wife. Although it was mandatory for all citizens and schoolchildren to attend the Republic Day ceremonies organised at their respective places and schools, I suggested that we should not send our daughter to her school in Bhachau.

She was still very young, and the journey of nearly 45 kilometres each way for a ceremony of short duration would have been tiring for her.

More importantly, my driver—who had returned only around 4:30 a.m. after performing a strenuous duty of nearly twenty continuous hours—was in no condition to undertake another long drive.

After this discussion, we went to sleep, knowing that in any case I would have to attend the flag-hoisting ceremony and attend to other responsibilities at the project site later that morning.

When we woke up around 7:30 a.m., we conveyed our decision to our little daughter. She accepted it quietly, though she was clearly unhappy, having lost the opportunity to meet her friends and spend time with them at school.

Later, after the earthquake struck, we came to know that the building of St Xavier's School had collapsed and that a few innocent children had lost their lives, along with several others.

The very thought was terrifying—that children who had gone out to attend a Republic Day ceremony never returned to their parents or their homes.

One could only empathise and try to console the grief-stricken parents who lost their children in a matter of seconds. Even a classmate of my daughter was among those who perished in the collapse.

Once again, it felt as though God Himself had given me a silent hint that night. Had that thought not crossed my mind, the outcome could have been far worse—something so painful and unbearable that it would have been impossible for us to live with.

Some moments are not decisions of the mind, but whispers of fate—and their meaning is understood only in hindsight.

Incident 3 – An Unseen Hand at Work

Had we not decided to continue work on 26th January, the consequences could have been disastrous. Ordinarily, on a holiday, the workers would have remained inside their dormitories until late morning.

Had they been within the labour colony when the earthquake struck, the loss of life would have been immense and unimaginable.

Although it is generally unacceptable to ask workers to report for duty on a holiday, this decision—taken under unavoidable circumstances—proved to be life-saving.

At that moment, it was merely a call taken in the interest of work continuity; in hindsight, it stood as a shield against tragedy.

Once again, it strengthened my belief that at critical moments, unseen forces quietly guide human decisions towards a greater purpose—often revealing their meaning only after danger has passed.

Chapter Eight

Life After the Earthquake

The devastation left behind by the earthquake was overwhelming. Once the immediate shock subsided, we were confronted with the harsh reality of rebuilding our lives amidst destruction. The path ahead was uncertain, yet we knew we had no choice but to move forward.

Despite the chaos, my foremost responsibility was to ensure the safety of my family, my team, and everyone associated with the project. At the same time, the continuity of work had to be maintained. However, the challenges were immense.

Continuous aftershocks created constant fear, and there was an acute shortage of essential supplies such as food, drinking water, and shelter. At times, it felt as though we were living in complete isolation from the outside world.

Keeping these challenges in mind, we formulated certain basic protocols to ensure safety and order:

- No one was allowed to enter damaged structures unless absolutely necessary.
- Everyone was instructed to sleep in open areas or tents during the night.

- Meals were prepared collectively to avoid wastage and ensure fairness.
- Similar safety measures were implemented in the labour colonies to protect workers and maintain discipline.

Life in Tents

Soon, we received the first consignment of essential groceries and cloth tents for shelter, as it had become impossible to stay inside our houses, which were already cracked and dangerously vulnerable to collapse due to frequent aftershocks.

The tents were distributed among all staff members and became our temporary homes for the months that followed. One by one, we erected these tents and began living in them—sleeping, cooking, and carrying on our daily lives under canvas roofs.

These tents remained our shelter until the day we were transferred from the project.

Presented below are the real photographs of the tents where we lived, cooked, and slept. They speak for themselves—silent yet powerful testimony to how we chose to endure extreme hardship together.

Despite the difficult conditions, not once did the thought of giving up cross our minds.

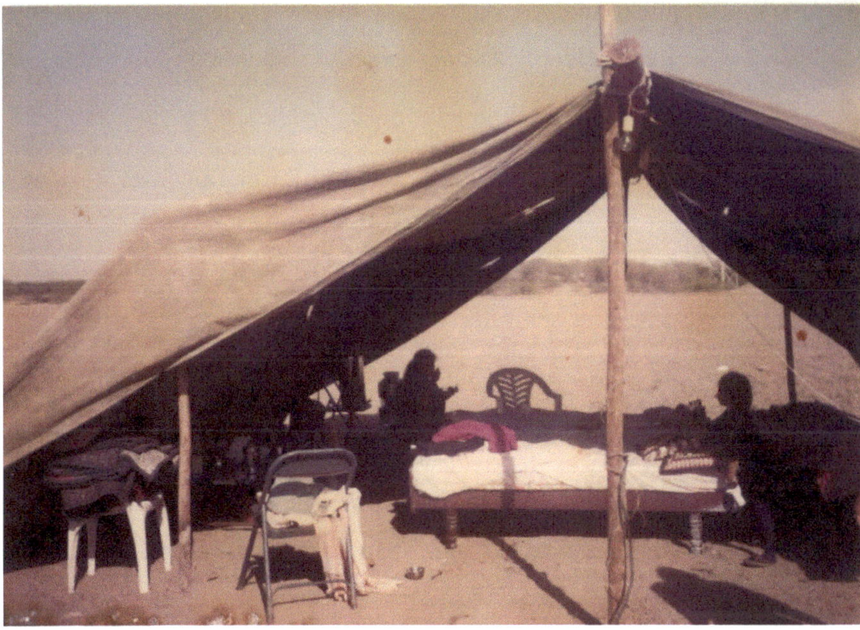

Fig:VIII.1

Fig:VIII.2

Despite the extreme conditions, the entire Gammon family stood united. Every individual contributed selflessly, putting collective responsibility above personal comfort.

Not a single person abandoned their duty except for one engineer who, overwhelmed by the hardships, chose to take leave and return home — never to come back. The spirit of teamwork and resilience during those days remains one of the most inspiring experiences of my life.

When Support Arrived from Afar

One of the most commendable gestures came from our Head Office. With due approval from senior management, immediate support was extended to the site. Mr. C. D. Desai, who was then Project Manager at one of our Mumbai projects, personally travelled to Suraj Bari carrying relief materials. His presence lifted morale and reinforced the belief that we were not alone in this difficult time.

Gradually, life began to find a rhythm again. Although aftershocks continued to occur and fear lingered in our minds, we adapted to the circumstances.

A Smile Amid the Tremors

One memory that still brings a faint smile is my daughter's instinctive reaction—each time a tremor occurred, she would run straight into the open ground without hesitation, as if guided by instinct.

In time, we learned to live with uncertainty, to rebuild not only structures but also confidence and hope. The adversity strengthened our resolve, and together we moved forward, determined to complete our mission despite all odds.

Chapter Nine

Restoration and Rebuilding

Before the earthquake struck, 37 out of the total 39 spans of the superstructure had already been completed. The remaining work involved erecting the I-girders for the final two spans and casting the deck slabs.

During the earthquake, the violent tremors caused significant displacement of the girders. Many of them shifted from their original positions, moving in different directions.

However, the presence of seismic barriers on either side of the pier caps prevented catastrophic collapse. Although these barriers were damaged, they successfully restricted excessive lateral movement of the spans.

Most of the neoprene bearings were damaged, while a few remained partially intact. Given the sensitivity of bearing performance in bridge behaviour, it became imperative to inspect every bearing thoroughly and replace those found defective. This required lifting the entire superstructure using heavy-duty hydraulic jacks — a complex and high-risk operation.

In coordination with the Head Office design team, a comprehensive restoration plan was prepared. This included:

- Detailed inspection of damages
- Preparation of repair and strengthening methodologies
- Identification of materials and specialised equipment required

Once the planning phase was completed, a specialised agency experienced in bridge restoration was mobilised from Mumbai. The team arrived with high-capacity hydraulic jacks and other specialised equipment required for the task.

After the arrival of the restoration team, a detailed joint inspection of the entire structure was carried out. Based on the findings, work was divided into multiple shifts, and round-the-clock operations commenced. The task ahead was enormous and demanded exceptional coordination, discipline, and technical precision.

As the Project Head, I was under immense pressure. The situation was being closely monitored not only by senior management but also by the Chief Minister's Office and the Prime Minister's Office, as the bridge served as the sole connectivity link to Kutch. Any delay would have severely impacted relief operations and public movement.

The movement of relief convoys had already been affected, with vehicles lined up for kilometres on the Morbi side. Restoring the bridge at the earliest was therefore critical for humanitarian as well as logistical reasons.

Erection of I-Girders

The erection of I-girders posed one of the greatest challenges. The workers were understandably hesitant to operate heavy cranes on a temporary jetty under the constant threat of aftershocks. Even a minor tremor could have destabilised the cranes and caused catastrophic consequences.

Recognising their fear, I made a conscious decision to lead from the front. Next day morning after reaching site we, the whole staff and erection team performed a big Pooja and then after I decided to stood beneath the span as the cranes prepared to lift the girder, reassuring the team and instilling confidence.

Though this act went against standard safety protocols, it was necessary to restore morale and overcome the paralyzing fear gripping the workforce.

Once the lifting commenced, the operation proceeded smoothly. One by one, the girders were placed successfully. The team's confidence grew, and momentum returned to the site.

Gradually, all remaining tasks were completed, including:

- Replacement of damaged neoprene bearings
- Epoxy grouting
- Reconstruction of approaches
- Realignment of displaced girders
- Casting of deck slabs and crash barriers
- Restoration of bituminous surfacing

Despite the emotional strain, exhaustion, and constant aftershocks, the team worked with unwavering commitment. The dedication shown by engineers, technicians, and workers alike was nothing short of extraordinary.

Completion of the Bridge

By the grace of God and the collective effort of everyone involved, the bridge was successfully restored and made traffic-worthy by **1st March 2001**.

I informed the Head Office and senior management that the bridge is ready for use. Considering the immense loss suffered by the region, it was decided that the opening would be kept low-key and dignified.

Accordingly, on **2nd March 2001**, a state transport bus plying between Bhachau and Morbi was allowed to cross the newly restored Suraj Bari Creek Bridge, marking the resumption of connectivity. Soon after, normal traffic flow resumed, while repair work on the older bridge continued.

Fig:IX.1 (Concept visualization created using AI)

Chapter Ten

A Feeling of Satisfaction

After the completion of the bridge and its opening to traffic on **2nd March 2001**, I reflected deeply on the journey that had led us there.

It is worth mentioning that the original scheduled date for completion was **4th March 2001**, and despite the devastation caused by the earthquake, we successfully completed the project **two days ahead of schedule**.

This achievement remains one of the proudest moments of my professional life.

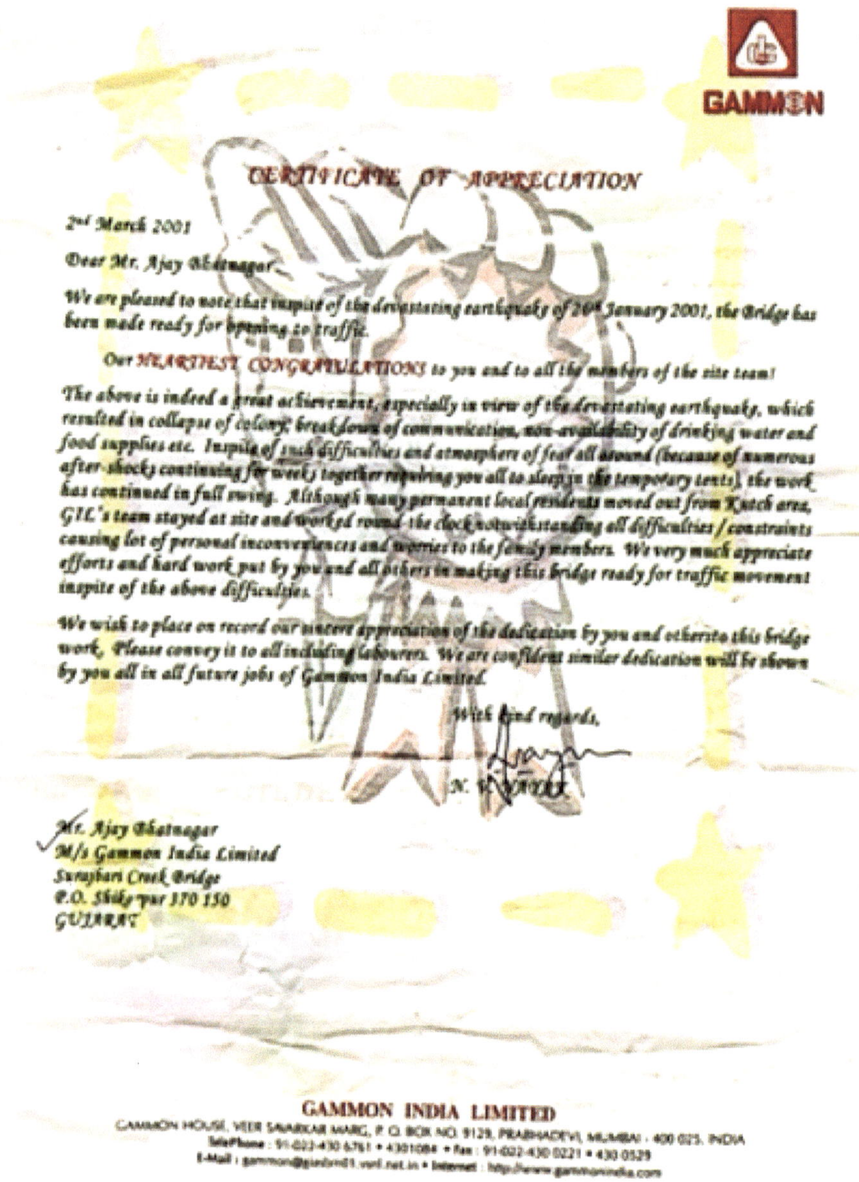

GAMMON

CERTIFICATE OF APPRECIATION

2nd March 2001

Dear Mr. Ajay Bhatnagar,

We are pleased to note that inspite of the devastating earthquake of 26th January 2001, the Bridge has been made ready for opening to traffic.

Our HEARTIEST CONGRATULATIONS to you and to all the members of the site team!

The above is indeed a great achievement, especially in view of the devastating earthquake, which resulted in collapse of colony, breakdown of communication, non-availability of drinking water and food supplies etc. Inspite of such difficulties and atmosphere of fear all around (because of numerous after-shocks continuing for weeks together requiring you all to sleep in the temporary tents), the work has continued in full swing. Although many permanent local residents moved out from Kutch area, GIL's team stayed at site and worked round the clock notwithstanding all difficulties / constraints causing lot of personal inconveniences and worries to the family members. We very much appreciate efforts and hard work put by you and all others in making this bridge ready for traffic movement inspite of the above difficulties.

We wish to place on record our sincere appreciation of the dedication by you and others to this bridge work. Please convey it to all including labourers. We are confident similer dedication will be shown by you all in all future jobs of Gammon India Limited.

With kind regards,

N. K[illegible]

Mr. Ajay Bhatnagar
M/s Gammon India Limited
Surajbari Creek Bridge
P.O. Shikarpur 370 150
GUJARAT

GAMMON INDIA LIMITED
GAMMON HOUSE, VEER SAVARKAR MARG, P. O. BOX NO. 9129, PRABHADEVI, MUMBAI - 400 025. INDIA
TelePhone : 91-022-430 6761 • 4301084 • Fax : 91-022-430 0221 • 430 0529
E-Mail : gammon@[illegible].net.in • Internet : http://www.gammonindia.com

Fig:X.1

This success was possible only because of the tireless efforts and unwavering dedication of every individual involved.

The workers, staff members, engineers, and supporting teams stood united through unimaginable hardship.

Their commitment, resilience, and sense of responsibility turned an impossible situation into a remarkable achievement.

I still vividly remember the visits of senior government officials, including dignitaries from the Chief Minister's office, who arrived to review the progress of the reconstruction work.

On several occasions, even the Honourable Chief Minister personally visited the site through chopper.

Their presence boosted morale and reaffirmed the importance of our collective mission.

A Celebration After the Storm

Before moving on to my next assignment, and soon after the bridge was opened to traffic, we decided to celebrate the festival of **Holi** with the entire staff. This celebration was far more than a ritual of colours—it was a heartfelt release after months of tension, hardship, and relentless effort.

It was our way of rejoicing in the greatest achievement the Gammon family had accomplished together, standing firm through the harshest of circumstances.

To mark this joyous milestone, we planned a **picnic-cum-Holi** trip to **Diu**. Together, we travelled, laughed, played with colours, and shared moments of unrestrained happiness.

The air was filled with cheer, music, and camaraderie. For a while, worries were forgotten, and what remained was pure joy, gratitude, and togetherness.

Those moments in Diu were not just a celebration of a festival, but a celebration of life, resilience, and unity—a reminder that even after the darkest times, colours always return.

Fig:X.2

Fig:X.3

Fig:X.4

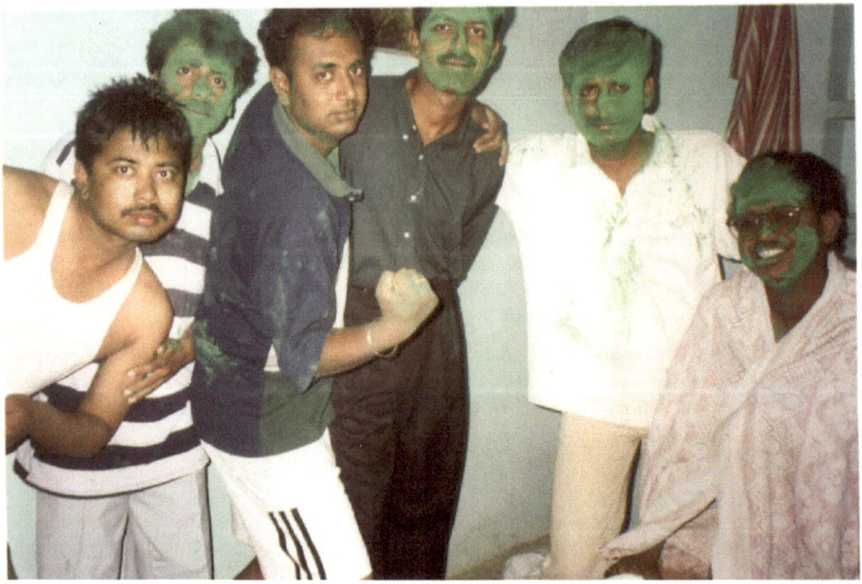

Fig X.5

A New Chapter Begins

After the successful opening of the bridge on 2nd March 2001, it was time for me to move on to the next chapter of my professional journey.

Before leaving Suraj Bari on 21st March 2001, I was overwhelmed by the affection, respect, and gratitude expressed by the workers, staff members, and local residents. Those moments remain deeply etched in my heart.

There is a unique sense of fulfilment that comes from completing a challenging project under extreme conditions. The satisfaction derived from overcoming adversity, serving the nation, and delivering results against all odds is something that cannot be measured or replaced.

The Organisation

The slogan of **M/s Gammon India Limited — "Builders to the Nation"** — truly reflected our mission. As civil engineers, we move from one project to another, contributing to the nation's growth and development.

From West Bengal to Gujarat and later to Assam, each assignment became a chapter of learning, resilience, and service.

I carry with me immense pride and gratitude for the opportunity to be part of such transformative work.

The memories, lessons, and bonds formed during this journey will remain with me forever.

Chapter Eleven

Reflections from a Life's Journey

As I bring this journey to a close, I find myself reflecting on the long road I have travelled — a path filled with challenges, learning, and countless moments that shaped not only my career but also my character.

This book is my humble attempt to put into words the experiences I lived through during my professional life.

Every incident described here is rooted in reality, drawn from moments that tested my endurance, my values, and my belief in perseverance.

I have tried to present these experiences with honesty, sincerity, and respect for all those who were part of the journey.

Over the span of more than three decades in the field, I witnessed both triumphs and trials — moments of pride as well as moments of deep uncertainty.

Each project, each responsibility, and each challenge added a new layer of understanding and strengthened my resolve as an engineer and as a human being.

Fig:XI.1 (Concept visualization created using AI)

If this book succeeds in offering insight, inspiration, or encouragement to even a single reader, then I will consider my effort worthwhile.

My hope is that these experiences may guide or motivate young professionals who aspire to build their careers with dedication, integrity, and resilience.

As I look back, I feel a deep sense of gratitude — towards my family, my colleagues, my mentors, and everyone who walked alongside me on this journey.

The lessons learned, the bonds formed, and the memories created will remain with me for a lifetime.

This book is not just a record of events; it is a reflection of a life shaped by commitment, responsibility, and faith in perseverance.

About the author

Ajay Bhatnagar, a Civil Engineer by profession, born and brought up in a small town in Uttar Pradesh, North India. After completing my intermediate education from Rampur, Uttar Pradesh. I pursued my Bachelor's Degree in Engineering from Pune University in year 1990.

I began my professional career with one of India's most reputed construction company, **M/s Gammon India Limited**. From April 1991 onwards, I worked on several major infrastructure projects across different states, including Rajasthan, Karnataka, West Bengal, Gujarat, Assam, Odisha, Maharashtra, and Uttar Pradesh. Over a span of nearly eighteen years, I served in various capacities—from Junior Engineer to Project Manager—gaining invaluable experience, recognition, and professional growth.

During these years, I had the opportunity to work on diverse projects such as highways, dams, commercial buildings, flyovers, creek bridges, rail bridges, and river bridges etc. Each assignment brought new challenges and learning opportunities. I was fortunate to work under several experienced and accomplished project managers who not only guided me professionally but also instilled in me the confidence to handle complex responsibilities independently.

One of the most significant milestones of my career was my association with the Suraj Bari Creek Bridge project. At a relatively young age, I was entrusted with the responsibility of Project Manager—a role that shaped my professional identity and tested my capabilities to the fullest.

What unfolds in these pages has left a lasting imprint on me, influencing the person I have become and sharpening my awareness of how precarious, yet enduring, life can be.